Into the BLUE
A Counting Adventure

by Amy Foos Kapoor

Illustrated by Jennifer Ard

BEALU BOOKS

new voices for curious readers

Main Text of the Story
Copyright 2025 by Amy Foos Kapoor

Illustrations
Copyright 2025 by Jennifer Ard

ISBN Hardcover: 978-1-962981-22-4
ISBN Paperback: 978-1-962981-23-1
ISBN eBook: 978-1-962981-47-7

Library of Congress Control Number: 2024950926
Publisher's Cataloging-in-Publication Data is on file with the publisher.

Written by: Amy Foos Kapoor
Illustrated by: Jennifer Ard
Edited by: Precious McKenzie
Book cover and interior design by Tara Raymo • creativelytara.com

Printed in the United States of America
November 2024

BeaLu Books
Tampa, Florida

www.BeaLuBooks.com

"For my adventurous sons
Jared Michael and Rihaan Phillip"
—Amy Foos Kapoor

Into the BLUE

A Counting Adventure

by Amy Foos Kapoor

Illustrated by Jennifer Ard

"**One** shell,
two buckets,
three umbrellas.
How many things can
you count?" asked Nana.

Jon loved a counting challenge. He hopped across the hot, sugary beach.

Foaming waves crashed onto the shore.

When the waves withdrew, Jon uncovered a special shell. "**One** sand-dollar."

Then, he spotted furry fruit
up in a palm tree.
"TWO coconuts."

Across the sparkling sea,
Jon watched the wide horizon.
"**Three** sailboats."

Leaping above the waves,
a family flipped and played.
"**Four** dolphins, but one is a baby!"

The dolphins dove out of sight.
Jon wondered about their world under the sea.

He no longer wanted to count ordinary things.
Jon closed his eyes and imagined
swimming toward the friendly pod.

The baby dolphin splashed all around.
Jon petted her rubbery head, and she smiled.
"Click!" "Click!" "Click!"

Jon dove underwater and swam into the blue.
The salty water stung his eyes.
Flat fish cruised the sandy bottom
with their water wings.
"**Five** stingrays."

Jon followed a beam of sunlight
toward a colorful coral reef.
Regal fish darted in and out
of waving sea fans.
"**Six** angelfish."

Spiky creatures hid inside rock crevices.
"**Seven** sea urchins."

Deeper into the sea,
Jon shuddered as the water
grew colder and darker.
Green-shelled giants paddled
through the chilly currents.
"**Eight** sea turtles."
Something silvery with jagged teeth
caught Jon's eye.

"**Nine** hammerhead sharks."
And they were heading his way!
The dolphin family rushed to his side.
The baby nudged Jon.

Up! Up! Up!

Jon broke through the water's surface
and took a big breath.
The sun warmed his face.

Above the crested waves,
   the pod leaped and led Jon safely to shore.
"Click!" "Click!" "Click!"

Jon opened his eyes.

His imaginary adventure was done!

Soaring birds squawked

through the drifting clouds.

"Ten seagulls."

Jon ran back through
the hot, sugary sand.

He told Nana all about
the things he had counted.
Ten seagulls.
Nine hammerhead sharks.
Eight sea turtles.
Seven sea urchins.
Six angelfish.
Five stingrays.
Four dolphins.
Three sailboats.
Two coconuts.
And **one** sand-dollar.

"What an amazing adventure," she said.
"Next time, we'll see what you can
count at the planetarium."
Jon imagined a star-filled sky.

Fun Facts

Angelfish. Marine angelfish are brightly colored and seen among tropical reefs in both the Atlantic and the Indo-Pacific Oceans. As omnivores, they eat sponges, algae, sea fans, soft corals and jellyfish. Their bright colorful patterns give them camouflage from predators.

Coconut Palm Trees are found throughout the tropics in warm, coastal areas. It is a single-trunk palm with massive feather-like leaves that can grow up to 80 feet (24 meters) tall. The tree produces coconuts which are one of the most popular fruits in the world.

Coral reefs are known as the "rainforests of the sea" and are the most diverse of all marine ecosystems. The animals responsible for building these reefs are corals. They have a durable exoskeleton which makes up the underwater structures while protecting their soft bodies. There are also soft corals which are flexible organisms that often look like plants and trees such as sea fans and sea whips. Corals feed by catching small marine life like fish and plankton with their stinging tentacles or through algae, called zooxanthellae, that provides energy through photo synthesis with sunlight. There are four categories of coral reef: fringing reefs, barrier reefs, patch reefs and atolls.

Dolphins. There are many species of dolphin throughout the world. Dolphins are often heard clicking, which is the sonar system that they use for navigation, hunting, and avoiding predators. Dolphins live in groups called "pods" which have anywhere from two to 30 members.

Hammerhead Sharks are the most distinctive of all sharks because of their unique T-shaped heads that resemble a hammer. Scientists believe the extended position of its eyes at each side of its head gives it a wider field of view and helps with depth perception. They also form groups or "schools" of up to 500 members, which is unusual for sharks.

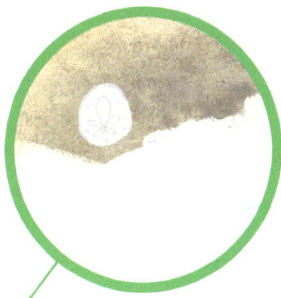

Sand Dollar. A sand dollar on the beach is the bleached skeleton of a deceased invertebrate marine animal known as an echinoderm, which is closely related to sea urchins and starfish. Living sand dollars have a flat, disk-shaped body covered in velvety textured spines with tiny hairs. They are well adapted for burrowing in the sand. Its mouth is located on the underside of the body. It uses its tiny spines for digging and crawling in order to find food like algae and decaying matter on the ocean floor. The sand dollar's surface has a pattern of five petals spreading out from the center.

Sea Urchins are commonly found along the rocky ocean floor and coral reefs. They are small with a round body with long, prickly spines that are used for protection, movement and capturing food. Beware of their venomous spikes because they can sting!

Sea Gulls. There is an abundance of sea gulls across the Northern Hemisphere. These adaptable opportunistic seabirds are mostly white and/or gray with some black markings, webbed feet with yellow hooked beaks. Gulls feed on a wide range of prey including fish, worms, grubs, insects, mollusks and are known to steal sandwiches and chips from beachgoers. They live in noisy groups called colonies and are very good parents.

Sea Turtles. There are seven species of sea turtles and the most common types in the Florida Keys are the Loggerhead, then the Green Sea Turtle, Hawksbill and Kemp's Ridley. The massive Loggerhead is the world's largest hard-shelled turtle weighing anywhere from 180 to 440 pounds (82 kilograms to 200 kilograms). These reptiles are air-breathing and live most of their lives swimming in the ocean. The only time they come on land is when females lay eggs during the nesting season on the beach.

Stingrays are fish that have flat, disk-shaped bodies with five gill openings and the mouth on its underside with long, sharp spines on their whip-like tails which are venomous. Their large wing-like pectoral fins extend forward along the sides of the head and gills. They inhabit warm temperate and tropical waters. Stingrays are bottom dwellers and often lie partially buried in the shallows with sand covering them.

About the Author

Amy Foos Kapoor is a children's book author and an independent producer of film, television, and digital media. She has an MFA from Spalding University's Naslund-Mann School of Writing. Amy lives in Louisville, Kentucky, with her husband, two sons, and two Corgis. She enjoys going on grand adventures with her family which has been a great source of inspiration for her stories.

About the Illustrator

Jennifer Ard is a children's book author and illustrator from Laurel, Montana. Her favorite stories to work on are those that have a little bit of science, some humor, and a lot of heart or those stories that shed light on misunderstood or under-appreciated creatures. When she is not writing and painting, you can find her attempting to grow food, attempting to identify bugs, and spending time with her incredibly supportive family. See her current work on her website at jenniferard.com.

Author's Note and Websites to Visit

All of the animal and plant species in this book live off the coasts of Florida, where I've spent lots of time with my two sons who both have a great and curious love of the ocean.

The following websites were very helpful in learning more about these wondrous creatures and plants:

"Facts About Sea Urchins in The Florida Keys." Key West Aquarium, 2 June 2020, www.keywestaquarium.com/sea-urchins.

"Kids-World-Travel-Guide." www.kids-world-travel-guide.com/philippines-facts.html.

"The Sharks of Florida: Meet the Sharks." Florida Shark Diving, floridasharkdiving.com/florida-shark-diving-the-sharks/.

"Stingrays." National Geographic, 24 Sept. 2018, www.nationalgeographic.com/animals/fish/group/stingrays/.

www.ingramcontent.com/pod-product-compliance
Lightning Source LLC
Chambersburg PA
CBHW061149030426
42335CB00003B/166